One Day at a Time

NEW NOMADS
NOTEBOOKS | PLANNERS | JOURNALS

Fellow Travelers on the Path to Recovery

Follow Us on Twitter: @NewNomadsPress

Visit Our Website for other Titles

https://press.new-nomads.com

One Day at a Time – Today Is:

Devotion/Affirmation	Meeting Schedule

Steps for Today	Courage

Success	Out of Self

Keep It Simple

Feeling: H A L T

What's Important Today?

Talk to My Sponsor About

Progress, Not Perfection

Find Serenity

One Day at a Time – Today Is:

Devotion/Affirmation	Meeting Schedule

Steps for Today	Courage

Success	Out of Self

Live In Today

Feeling: H A L T

What's Important Today?

Talk to My Sponsor About

Progress, Not Perfection

Work The Steps

One Day at a Time – Today Is:

Devotion/Affirmation	Meeting Schedule

Steps for Today	Courage

Success	Out of Self

Love Yourself (and Like Yourself)

Feeling: H A L T

What's Important Today?

Talk to My Sponsor About

Progress, Not Perfection

Find Hope In Today

One Day at a Time – Today Is:

Devotion/Affirmation	Meeting Schedule

Steps for Today	Courage

Success	Out of Self

Accept the Things I Cannot Change

Feeling: H A L T

What's Important Today?

Talk to My Sponsor About

Progress, Not Perfection

Find Happiness in Simplicity

One Day at a Time – Today Is:

Devotion/Affirmation	Meeting Schedule

Steps for Today	Courage

Success	Out of Self

Be Honest

Feeling: H A L T

What's Important Today?

Talk to My Sponsor About

Progress, Not Perfection

Work The Steps

One Day at a Time – Today Is:

Devotion/Affirmation	Meeting Schedule

Steps for Today	Courage

Success	Out of Self

Let It Go

Feeling: H   A   L   T

What's Important Today?

Talk to My Sponsor About

Progress, Not Perfection

Surrender To Win

One Day at a Time – Today Is:

Devotion/Affirmation	Meeting Schedule

Steps for Today	Courage

Success	Out of Self

Keep It Simple

Feeling: H   A   L   T

What's Important Today?

Talk to My Sponsor About

Progress, Not Perfection

Find Serenity

One Day at a Time – Today Is:

Devotion/Affirmation	Meeting Schedule

Steps for Today	Courage

Success	Out of Self

Live In Today

Feeling: H   A   L   T

What's Important Today?

Talk to My Sponsor About

Progress, Not Perfection

Work The Steps

One Day at a Time – Today Is:

Devotion/Affirmation	Meeting Schedule

Steps for Today	Courage

Success	Out of Self

Love Yourself (and Like Yourself)

Feeling: H   A   L   T

What's Important Today?

Talk to My Sponsor About

Progress, Not Perfection

Find Hope In Today

One Day at a Time – Today Is:

Devotion/Affirmation	Meeting Schedule

Steps for Today	Courage

Success	Out of Self

Accept the Things I Cannot Change

Feeling: H   A   L   T

What's Important Today?

Talk to My Sponsor About

Progress, Not Perfection

Find Happiness in Simplicity

One Day at a Time – Today Is:

Devotion/Affirmation	Meeting Schedule

Steps for Today	Courage

Success	Out of Self

Be Honest

Feeling: H A L T

What's Important Today?

Talk to My Sponsor About

Progress, Not Perfection

Work The Steps

One Day at a Time – Today Is:

Devotion/Affirmation	Meeting Schedule

Steps for Today	Courage

Success	Out of Self

Let It Go

Feeling: H A L T

What's Important Today?

Talk to My Sponsor About

Progress, Not Perfection

Surrender To Win

One Day at a Time – Today Is:

Devotion/Affirmation	Meeting Schedule

Steps for Today	Courage

Success	Out of Self

Keep It Simple

Feeling: H A L T

What's Important Today?

Talk to My Sponsor About

Progress, Not Perfection

Find Serenity

One Day at a Time – Today Is:

Devotion/Affirmation	Meeting Schedule

Steps for Today	Courage

Success	Out of Self

Live In Today

Feeling: H A L T

What's Important Today?

Talk to My Sponsor About

Progress, Not Perfection

Work The Steps

One Day at a Time – Today Is:

Devotion/Affirmation	Meeting Schedule

Steps for Today	Courage

Success	Out of Self

Love Yourself (and Like Yourself)

Feeling: H   A   L   T

What's Important Today?

Talk to My Sponsor About

Progress, Not Perfection

Find Hope In Today

One Day at a Time – Today Is:

Devotion/Affirmation	Meeting Schedule

Steps for Today	Courage

Success	Out of Self

Accept the Things I Cannot Change

Feeling: H A L T

What's Important Today?

Talk to My Sponsor About

Progress, Not Perfection

Find Happiness in Simplicity

One Day at a Time – Today Is:

Devotion/Affirmation	Meeting Schedule

Steps for Today	Courage

Success	Out of Self

Be Honest

Feeling: H A L T

What's Important Today?

Talk to My Sponsor About

Progress, Not Perfection

Work The Steps

One Day at a Time – Today Is:

Devotion/Affirmation	Meeting Schedule

Steps for Today	Courage

Success	Out of Self

Let It Go

Feeling: H   A   L   T

What's Important Today?

Talk to My Sponsor About

Progress, Not Perfection

Surrender To Win

One Day at a Time – Today Is:

Devotion/Affirmation	Meeting Schedule

Steps for Today	Courage

Success	Out of Self

Keep It Simple

Feeling: H   A   L   T

What's Important Today?

Talk to My Sponsor About

Progress, Not Perfection

Find Serenity

One Day at a Time – Today Is:

Devotion/Affirmation	Meeting Schedule

Steps for Today	Courage

Success	Out of Self

Live In Today

Feeling: H A L T

What's Important Today?

Talk to My Sponsor About

Progress, Not Perfection

Work The Steps

One Day at a Time – Today Is:

Devotion/Affirmation	Meeting Schedule

Steps for Today	Courage

Success	Out of Self

Love Yourself (and Like Yourself)

Feeling: H A L T

What's Important Today?

Talk to My Sponsor About

Progress, Not Perfection

Find Hope In Today

One Day at a Time – Today Is:

Devotion/Affirmation	Meeting Schedule

Steps for Today	Courage

Success	Out of Self

Accept the Things I Cannot Change

Feeling: H A L T

What's Important Today?

Talk to My Sponsor About

Progress, Not Perfection

Find Happiness in Simplicity

One Day at a Time – Today Is:

Devotion/Affirmation	Meeting Schedule

Steps for Today	Courage

Success	Out of Self

Be Honest

Feeling: H   A   L   T

What's Important Today?

Talk to My Sponsor About

Progress, Not Perfection

Work The Steps

One Day at a Time – Today Is:

Devotion/Affirmation	Meeting Schedule

Steps for Today	Courage

Success	Out of Self

Let It Go

Feeling: H A L T

What's Important Today?

Talk to My Sponsor About

Progress, Not Perfection

Surrender To Win

One Day at a Time – Today Is:

Devotion/Affirmation	Meeting Schedule

Steps for Today	Courage

Success	Out of Self

Keep It Simple

Feeling: H   A   L   T

What's Important Today?

Talk to My Sponsor About

Progress, Not Perfection

Find Serenity

One Day at a Time – Today Is:

Devotion/Affirmation	Meeting Schedule

Steps for Today	Courage

Success	Out of Self

Live In Today

Feeling: H   A   L   T

What's Important Today?

Talk to My Sponsor About

Progress, Not Perfection

Work The Steps

One Day at a Time – Today Is:

Devotion/Affirmation	Meeting Schedule

Steps for Today	Courage

Success	Out of Self

Love Yourself (and Like Yourself)

Feeling: H   A   L   T

What's Important Today?

Talk to My Sponsor About

Progress, Not Perfection

Find Hope In Today

One Day at a Time – Today Is:

Devotion/Affirmation	Meeting Schedule

Steps for Today	Courage

Success	Out of Self

Accept the Things I Cannot Change

Feeling: H A L T

What's Important Today?

Talk to My Sponsor About

Progress, Not Perfection

Find Happiness in Simplicity

One Day at a Time – Today Is:

Devotion/Affirmation	Meeting Schedule

Steps for Today	Courage

Success	Out of Self

Be Honest

Feeling: H A L T

What's Important Today?

Talk to My Sponsor About

Progress, Not Perfection

Work The Steps

One Day at a Time – Today Is:

Devotion/Affirmation	Meeting Schedule

Steps for Today	Courage

Success	Out of Self

Let It Go

Feeling: H A L T

What's Important Today?

Talk to My Sponsor About

Progress, Not Perfection

Surrender To Win

One Day at a Time – Today Is:

Devotion/Affirmation	Meeting Schedule

Steps for Today	Courage

Success	Out of Self

Keep It Simple

Feeling: H   A   L   T

What's Important Today?

Talk to My Sponsor About

Progress, Not Perfection

Find Serenity

One Day at a Time – Today Is:

Devotion/Affirmation	Meeting Schedule

Steps for Today	Courage

Success	Out of Self

Live In Today

Feeling: H A L T

What's Important Today?

Talk to My Sponsor About

Progress, Not Perfection

Work The Steps

One Day at a Time – Today Is:

Devotion/Affirmation	Meeting Schedule

Steps for Today	Courage

Success	Out of Self

Love Yourself (and Like Yourself)

Feeling: H A L T

What's Important Today?

Talk to My Sponsor About

Progress, Not Perfection

Find Hope In Today

One Day at a Time – Today Is:

Devotion/Affirmation	Meeting Schedule

Steps for Today	Courage

Success	Out of Self

Accept the Things I Cannot Change

Feeling: H   A   L   T

What's Important Today?

Talk to My Sponsor About

Progress, Not Perfection

Find Happiness in Simplicity

One Day at a Time – Today Is:

Devotion/Affirmation	Meeting Schedule

Steps for Today	Courage

Success	Out of Self

Be Honest

Feeling: H   A   L   T

What's Important Today?

Talk to My Sponsor About

Progress, Not Perfection

Work The Steps

One Day at a Time – Today Is:

Devotion/Affirmation	Meeting Schedule

Steps for Today	Courage

Success	Out of Self

Let It Go

Feeling: H A L T

What's Important Today?

Talk to My Sponsor About

Progress, Not Perfection

Surrender To Win

One Day at a Time – Today Is:

Devotion/Affirmation	Meeting Schedule

Steps for Today	Courage

Success	Out of Self

Keep It Simple

Feeling: H A L T

What's Important Today?

Talk to My Sponsor About

Progress, Not Perfection

Find Serenity

One Day at a Time – Today Is:

Devotion/Affirmation	Meeting Schedule

Steps for Today	Courage

Success	Out of Self

Live In Today

Feeling: H A L T

What's Important Today?

Talk to My Sponsor About

Progress, Not Perfection

Work The Steps

One Day at a Time – Today Is:

Devotion/Affirmation	Meeting Schedule

Steps for Today	Courage

Success	Out of Self

Love Yourself (and Like Yourself)

Feeling: H   A   L   T

What's Important Today?

Talk to My Sponsor About

Progress, Not Perfection

Find Hope In Today

One Day at a Time – Today Is:

Devotion/Affirmation	Meeting Schedule

Steps for Today	Courage

Success	Out of Self

Accept the Things I Cannot Change

Feeling: H A L T

What's Important Today?

Talk to My Sponsor About

Progress, Not Perfection

Find Happiness in Simplicity

One Day at a Time – Today Is:

Devotion/Affirmation	Meeting Schedule

Steps for Today	Courage

Success	Out of Self

Be Honest

Feeling: H A L T

What's Important Today?

Talk to My Sponsor About

Progress, Not Perfection

Work The Steps

One Day at a Time – Today Is:

Devotion/Affirmation	Meeting Schedule

Steps for Today	Courage

Success	Out of Self

Let It Go

Feeling: H A L T

What's Important Today?

Talk to My Sponsor About

Progress, Not Perfection

Surrender To Win

One Day at a Time – Today Is:

Devotion/Affirmation	Meeting Schedule

Steps for Today	Courage

Success	Out of Self

Keep It Simple

Feeling: H A L T

What's Important Today?

Talk to My Sponsor About

Progress, Not Perfection

Find Serenity

One Day at a Time – Today Is:

Devotion/Affirmation	Meeting Schedule

Steps for Today	Courage

Success	Out of Self

Live In Today

Feeling: H A L T

What's Important Today?

Talk to My Sponsor About

Progress, Not Perfection

Work The Steps

One Day at a Time – Today Is:

Devotion/Affirmation	Meeting Schedule

Steps for Today	Courage

Success	Out of Self

Love Yourself (and Like Yourself)

Feeling: H   A   L   T

What's Important Today?

Talk to My Sponsor About

Progress, Not Perfection

Find Hope In Today

One Day at a Time – Today Is:

Devotion/Affirmation	Meeting Schedule

Steps for Today	Courage

Success	Out of Self

Accept the Things I Cannot Change

Feeling: H A L T

What's Important Today?

Talk to My Sponsor About

Progress, Not Perfection

Find Happiness in Simplicity

One Day at a Time – Today Is:

Devotion/Affirmation	Meeting Schedule

Steps for Today	Courage

Success	Out of Self

Be Honest

Feeling: H A L T

What's Important Today?

Talk to My Sponsor About

Progress, Not Perfection

Work The Steps

One Day at a Time – Today Is:

Devotion/Affirmation	Meeting Schedule

Steps for Today	Courage

Success	Out of Self

Let It Go

Feeling: H A L T

What's Important Today?

Talk to My Sponsor About

Progress, Not Perfection

Surrender To Win

One Day at a Time – Today Is:

Devotion/Affirmation	Meeting Schedule

Steps for Today	Courage

Success	Out of Self

Keep It Simple

Feeling: H A L T

What's Important Today?

Talk to My Sponsor About

Progress, Not Perfection

Find Serenity

One Day at a Time – Today Is:

Devotion/Affirmation	Meeting Schedule

Steps for Today	Courage

Success	Out of Self

Live In Today

Feeling: H   A   L   T

What's Important Today?

Talk to My Sponsor About

Progress, Not Perfection

Work The Steps

One Day at a Time – Today Is:

Devotion/Affirmation	Meeting Schedule

Steps for Today	Courage

Success	Out of Self

Love Yourself (and Like Yourself)

Feeling: H   A   L   T

What's Important Today?

Talk to My Sponsor About

Progress, Not Perfection

Find Hope In Today

One Day at a Time – Today Is:

Devotion/Affirmation	Meeting Schedule

Steps for Today	Courage

Success	Out of Self

Accept the Things I Cannot Change

Feeling: H   A   L   T

What's Important Today?

Talk to My Sponsor About

Progress, Not Perfection

Find Happiness in Simplicity

One Day at a Time – Today Is:

Devotion/Affirmation	Meeting Schedule

Steps for Today	Courage

Success	Out of Self

Be Honest

Feeling: H A L T

What's Important Today?

Talk to My Sponsor About

Progress, Not Perfection

Work The Steps

One Day at a Time – Today Is:

Devotion/Affirmation	Meeting Schedule

Steps for Today	Courage

Success	Out of Self

Let It Go

Feeling: H   A   L   T

What's Important Today?

Talk to My Sponsor About

Progress, Not Perfection

Surrender To Win

One Day at a Time – Today Is:

Devotion/Affirmation	Meeting Schedule

Steps for Today	Courage

Success	Out of Self

Keep It Simple

Feeling: H A L T

What's Important Today?

Talk to My Sponsor About

Progress, Not Perfection

Find Serenity

One Day at a Time – Today Is:

Devotion/Affirmation	Meeting Schedule

Steps for Today	Courage

Success	Out of Self

Live In Today

Feeling: H A L T

What's Important Today?

Talk to My Sponsor About

Progress, Not Perfection

Work The Steps

One Day at a Time – Today Is:

Devotion/Affirmation	Meeting Schedule

Steps for Today	Courage

Success	Out of Self

Love Yourself (and Like Yourself)

Feeling: H   A   L   T

What's Important Today?

Talk to My Sponsor About

Progress, Not Perfection

Find Hope In Today

One Day at a Time – Today Is:

Devotion/Affirmation	Meeting Schedule

Steps for Today	Courage

Success	Out of Self

Accept the Things I Cannot Change

Feeling: H   A   L   T

What's Important Today?

Talk to My Sponsor About

Progress, Not Perfection

Find Happiness in Simplicity

One Day at a Time – Today Is:

Devotion/Affirmation	Meeting Schedule

Steps for Today	Courage

Success	Out of Self

Be Honest

Feeling: H A L T

What's Important Today?

Talk to My Sponsor About

Progress, Not Perfection

Work The Steps

One Day at a Time – Today Is:

Devotion/Affirmation	Meeting Schedule

Steps for Today	Courage

Success	Out of Self

Let It Go

Feeling: H A L T

What's Important Today?

Talk to My Sponsor About

Progress, Not Perfection

Surrender To Win

Made in the USA
Monee, IL
28 February 2020